21st-CENTURY ECONOMICS

UNDERSTANDING
RECESSIONS

CHET'LA SEBREE

Cavendish
Square

New York

Published in 2020 by Cavendish Square Publishing, LLC
243 5th Avenue, Suite 136, New York, NY 10016

Copyright © 2020 by Cavendish Square Publishing, LLC

First Edition

Library of Congress Cataloging-in-Publication Data

Names: Sebree, Chet'la, author.
Title: Understanding recessions / Chet'la Sebree.
Description: First edition. | New York : Cavendish Square, 2020. |
Series: 21st-century economics | Includes bibliographical references and index.
Identifiers: LCCN 2018054845 (print) | LCCN 2018057707 (ebook) |
ISBN 9781502646040 (ebook) | ISBN 9781502646033 (library bound) |
ISBN 9781502646026 (pbk).
Subjects: LCSH: Recessions--Juvenile literature. |
Business cycles--Juvenile literature.
Classification: LCC HB3711 (ebook) | LCC HB3711 .S438 2020 (print) |
DDC 338.5/42--dc23
LC record available at https://lccn.loc.gov/2018054845

Portions of this book originally appeared in How
a Recession Works by Jeanne Nagle.

Editorial Director: David McNamara
Copy Editor: Nathan Heidelberger
Associate Art Director: Alan Sliwinski
Designer: Joseph Parenteau
Production Coordinator: Karol Szymczuk
Photo Research: J8 Media

The photographs in this book are used by permission and through the courtesy of:
Cover Pormezz/Shutterstock; Throughout book Champ008/Shutterstock; p. 4 E_Y_E/
iStock/Getty Images; p. 6 Bloomberg/Getty Images; p. 8 Tom Pennington/Getty Images;
p. 10 Art_girl/Shutterstock; p. 13 Thomas Barwick/DigitalVision/Getty Images; p. 14
Optigan13/Wikimedia Commons/File:Gross Domestic Product of California 2008 (millions
of current dollars).svg/CC PD; p. 18 John Holcroft/Ikon Images/Getty Images; p. 20
Toria/Shutterstock; p. 22 American Stock Archive/Getty Images; p. 24 robert cicchetti/
Shutterstock; p. 27 Dallas.Epperson/Wikimedia Commons/File:Simple supply and demand.
svg/CC BY-SA 3.0; p. 28 Rena Schild/Shutterstock; p. 31 POOL/AFP/Getty Images; p. 33
Spencer Platt/Getty Images; p. 36 traveler1116/iStock/Getty Images; p. 41 boonchai
wedmakawand/Moment/Getty Images; p. 42 Billion Photos/Getty Images; p. 47 Ridofranz/
iStock/Getty Images; p. 48 Joe Raedle/Getty Images; p. 52 klublu/Shutterstock; p. 53
Phelan M. Ebenhack/Bloomberg/Getty Images; p. 57 Cartoon Resource/Shutterstock;
p. 60 filadendron/E+/Getty Images; p. 63 The Navigators/Wikimedia Commons/
File:Economic Recovery sign Clean.png/CC BY-SA 3.0; p. 64 Library of Congress.

Printed in the United States of America

CONTENTS

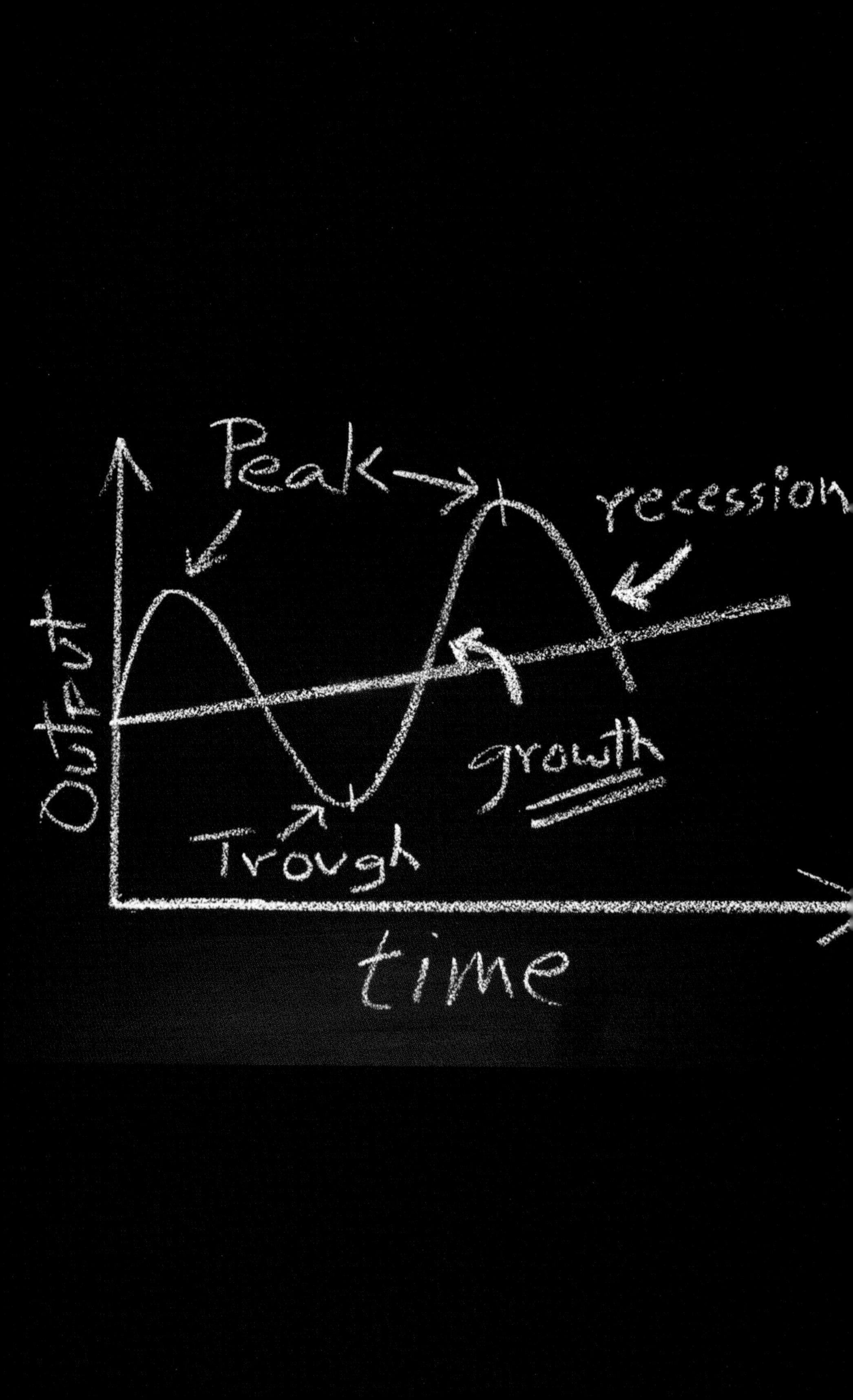
Peak
recession
Output
growth
Trough
time

THE BUSINESS CYCLE

Oceans follow a natural cycle. Water builds into a wave, which reaches a certain height before it crashes and recedes, or pulls back. Similarly, economies follow an ebb and flow called the business cycle. An economy expands and builds until it reaches a peak. The economy then contracts, or tightens, before it hits its bottom. Once it hits this bottom, the economy expands or builds again until it reaches a new peak. Recessions are the periods in which the economy contracts; they are a normal part of the cycle. Even though recessions are a part of the normal flow, they can still be very difficult for individuals, companies, and governments.

Opposite: The business cycle goes through four main periods: growth, peak, trough, and recession. Although it's a natural cycle, the length of each period varies.

Twenty-First-Century Recessions in the United States

The United States enjoyed some general prosperity during parts of the first decade of the twenty-first century. A large portion of the country's population either had plenty of

In 2008 alone, nearly one million people lost their home to foreclosure.

money or was able to borrow it easily from banks and other lending companies. People were not hesitant to spend what they had either. Using loans from banks and credit cards, people purchased many goods and services, especially expensive new houses.

After several years of this thriving economy, however, Americans started to sense a change in the economic atmosphere. Beginning in late 2006, there were signs of an economic slowdown. A slowdown is when the rate of economic activity decreases. It seemed that Americans had spent money faster than they could earn it. When the time came to return loans and pay off credit cards, many people found themselves deeply in debt. This made it hard for them to buy anything else, so their spending decreased. Other consumers noticed this, too, and became nervous that the same thing might happen to them. Therefore, they also cut way back on their spending. This led to the Great Recession (2007–2009).

The Effect of Recessions

Just the idea that a recession might be looming on the horizon is enough to put people on edge. That's because there are several negative effects associated with a slowdown in economic growth. During a recession, companies sell fewer goods and services. As a result, companies lay off workers because they no longer need

In periods of growth, people are willing and able to purchase what they need in addition to what they want. For instance, the Black Friday in 2009, after the economy began to recover from the Great Recession, saw a 4.7 percent increase in shoppers.

them or can no longer afford to pay them. A "layoff" is when a company fires an employee for financial reasons. Unfortunately, despite firing people to save money, some companies still go out of business. When people lose their jobs, the unemployment rate rises. When people are not working, they are less likely to spend money on goods and services, especially luxury items. This hurts businesses even more.

Although recessions can be frightening for everyone, it is important to remember they are a normal part of the business cycle. Understanding them can not only make them less scary but also help us better prepare for them.

CHAPTER 1

DEFINING RECESSIONS

Economies throughout the world revolve around the idea of "value." Something is considered valuable if it is precious or special. People want or need things that are considered valuable. In economic terms, an item's value can relate to the supply and demand for the object. When merchandise is rare or even one of a kind, like a famous artist's painting, it is considered valuable partly because there is a limited supply of this item. It is considered even more valuable if lots of people want the one painting. Conversely, poster reprints of the painting will usually have less value because these can be mass-produced, meaning the supply can be quite high.

Opposite: Grandidierite, pictured here, is one of the rarest and most expensive gemstones in the world. It can cost up to $20,000 per 200 milligrams.

Measuring a Country's Value

A recession happens when the value of what a country has to offer—to its own citizens and to other countries—decreases for at least several months. This is when an economy's normal buying and selling patterns slow down. In other words, people hold back from spending as much money as they normally would. This means that there is less of a demand for goods and services. As a result, businesses scale back on the products they make available for sale, also known as their supply of goods and services.

Buying and selling patterns are represented primarily by a country's gross domestic product (GDP). This figure represents the total value of goods and services produced by businesses within a country's borders during a given period of time. It is an economic indicator, which is a statistic. This type of statistic is used to predict a country's future economic trends. The GDP can be calculated by adding up all the money spent on goods and services in a country. It includes personal purchases like food and clothing, business investments, and government purchases. It also includes net exports. These are goods and services sold to other countries minus the goods and services purchased from other countries, also called imports. All goods and services created and offered in all fifty states, the District of Columbia, and the US territories are included in the United States' GDP.

Goods and services include everything from clothes and accessories to utilities like water and electricity.

Another economic statistic that refers to a country's total output is the gross national product (GNP). The GNP measures the total amount of goods and services produced by a country either within the country or abroad each year. So, for instance, the United States' GNP would include cars manufactured in foreign countries by American companies.

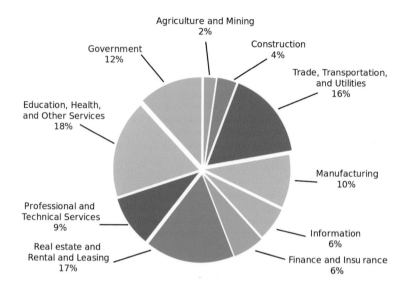

Agriculture and Mining
2%

Construction
4%

Government
12%

Trade, Transportation,
and Utilities
16%

Education, Health,
and Other Services
18%

Manufacturing
10%

Professional and
Technical Services
9%

Information
6%

Real estate and
Rental and Leasing
17%

Finance and Insu rance
6%

States, like countries, have gross domestic products. This pie chart represents the percentage of each industry that made up California's gross domestic product in 2008.

A Normal Business Cycle

What some people don't realize is that recessions are a normal part of the way the economy works. If you were to make a chart showing economic activity over the course of a year, it would look like a wavy line or a small mountain range with hills and valleys. That's because the business cycle goes through a series of ups, called peaks, and downs, known as troughs. When the cycle is on its way up, the economy is experiencing increased growth. It is said to be going through an expansion. The economy is said to go through a contraction when it is on its way down.

The contractions that happen during the normal business cycle are recessions. In a way, contractions are how the economy cools itself down after it has heated up and expanded too much. Expansions, likewise, are how the economy recovers and climbs back up after experiencing a trough. The economy works best when it has this moderate up-and-down motion. It is as if constantly changing creates a kind of balance and stability.

Over the course of a normal business cycle, the contractions, or recessions, usually are not too severe. They also often correct themselves fairly quickly. According to the National Bureau of Economic Research (NBER), recessions generally last, on average, about a year.

The Economic Domino Effect

Although economists often disagree on exactly when a recession has started, they do agree on how a recession acts once it has begun. First, and most important, the rate at which people spend money slows down. This slowdown may begin in only one business sector, or field of work, at first. Eventually, the lag in spending spreads to other sectors because the economy is interdependent. That means different types of businesses are connected, so what affects one business affects many others as well.

THE REGULATION OF RECESSIONS

Each nation assigns a government agency to keep track of the figures that make up the gross domestic product (GDP). In the United States, this task is the responsibility of the US Bureau of Economic Analysis.

During a recession, the numbers collected by the bureau show that the GDP is declining, or on a downward curve. This is also referred to as negative growth. When studying GDP trends, economists look at the "real GDP." This figure is different from the nominal GDP, the number that is calculated by adding up all money spent on goods and services. The real GDP is the nominal GDP adjusted to consider changes in the value of money. For instance, ten cents in the 1920s purchased far more than ten cents will purchase in the 2020s. By adjusting the GDP to account for these differences, economists can compare GDP levels from one year to the next, without worrying that changing price levels are misrepresenting the data.

This information is then used by the Federal Reserve, which is the country's central bank. Every three months, the Federal Reserve evaluates the GDP data from the previous three months. They use this data to predict where the economy is in the business cycle. Usually, the economy needs to move downward for at least six to nine months for there to be a recession. Sometimes, the GDP numbers are flat, remaining at about the same level for several months. This is a different economic phenomenon than a recession known as stagnation. Likewise, if a country experiences negative growth for only a quarter and then has positive growth the next two quarters, the economy is not considered to have been in a recession.

This image depicts how industries are interrelated. Financial problems in one sector can lead to issues in others.

This is called the domino effect. If you line up domino tiles and tip the first one over, it knocks over the next, which knocks over the next, and so on. Sectors of the economy react in much the same way during a recession. When one type of business topples, it usually shakes, and possibly completely knocks over, others.

For instance, if cars aren't selling well, then the manufacturer will not make as many vehicles. Car companies will then lay off workers because there isn't enough for them to do and the companies' costs need to be lowered. The unemployed auto workers no longer have enough money to buy things, such as new clothes. If enough people stop buying new clothes, the clothing industry experiences a slowdown in sales. This could result in layoffs in retail stores and textile manufacturing factories. A small clothing store may even lose enough sales that it is forced to go out of business, which means more people are unemployed. The more unemployed workers there are, the fewer people there are to strengthen the economy through consumer spending. This, in turn, leads to more pressure on stores and manufacturers, and to more layoffs.

This domino effect can have a much bigger impact than just on the business sectors of one country. While each nation has its own financial system that is managed independently, those systems are also interdependent. This means that they rely on each other for their well-being and smooth functioning, through a process known as economic globalization. This involves connections made between businesses and marketplaces around the world. Trade (imports and exports), foreign investments, and international banking are tools of economic globalization.

A Worldwide Effect

Just as economic slowdowns can spread from one business sector to another, a recession that starts in one country can affect the economies of financially interdependent nations. This can eventually cause a global recession. For instance, less spending in the United States doesn't lower only the United States' GDP. It also slows the economies of countries that export products to the United States. These countries depend on sales to the United States to boost their own economic activity. Without these sales, their economies suffer.

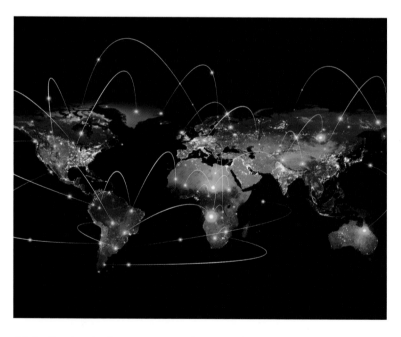

Globalization is the connection between businesses and marketplaces around the world.

During a global recession, there is a decline in the gross world product (GWP), or the global GDP. This figure represents the total monetary value of all goods and services produced around the world added together. The International Monetary Fund (IMF), a financial monitoring organization, uses several economic indicators to measure global recessions. These indicators include industrial production, trade, the movement of money between international economics, oil consumption, and unemployment rates. In 2009, the IMF predicted that the global economy would contract by 2.5 percent.

These types of recessions, however, are rare. They do not happen as regularly as the milder recessions that occur in a country's natural business cycle. The last global recession was from 2008 to 2009. Prior to that, the last global recession was in 1991. Thankfully, financial crises like these were only recessions. Though they affected a lot of people, they were less extreme than even worse financial crises called depressions.

Recession Versus Depression

You've probably heard of economic depressions in a history class in reference to the Great Depression. It was a financial crisis that lasted throughout much of the 1930s. Depressions, like recessions, are defined by a slowdown in the economy. However, the term "depression" is reserved for major economic declines. During them, people struggle to pay for basic necessities like food and shelter. Depressions are different from recessions in that they are not a part of the normal business cycle.

Economists use the GDP to help gauge whether a slowdown is a recession or a depression. A decline of less than 10 percent in the GDP is considered a recession. In the 1970s, the United States economy experienced a slowdown that economists agree was a recession. Over

During the Great Depression, so many people lost their jobs and homes that they were forced to build shacks out of whatever materials they could find, such as the barrels, baskets, cardboard boxes, and tires that make up roofs in this image.

two years, from 1973 to 1975, the country's GDP fell 3.6 percent. Similarly, during the Great Recession, the GDP fell by approximately 4 percent.

During the Great Depression, the GDP dropped about 30 percent at its lowest point. The impact of this financial crisis could be seen through homelessness and unemployment rates. People did whatever they could to survive, including living in temporary shacks and traveling from town to town to find work. Even as the economy was recovering during the 1930s, the decline in the GDP stayed above the 10 percent threshold. Like recessions, the Great Depression had a worldwide impact.

Lessons Learned

In many ways, governments around the world learned from the Great Depression. Many recessions since then have been saved from turning into depressions based on the lessons learned from the 1930s. Even still, it is important to understand how recessions happen in order to keep the economy in a healthy place.

CHAPTER 2

REASONS FOR RECESSIONS

There are many different factors that can cause a recession. Supply and demand have a direct effect on the business cycle. The relationship between the availability of products and people wanting to purchase those goods and services is responsible for the business cycle's expansions and contractions. That connection, along with events that pull on economic resources and the ways in which a nation's government handles its money supply, can ultimately determine whether or not a country experiences a recession.

Opposite: In 2014, thousands of people stood outside of Apple stores eagerly awaiting the release of the iPhone 6. In the months that followed, demand was so high that Apple could barely keep the phones in stock.

Supply and Demand

The law of supply and demand states that the value of a good or service changes according to how much of that given product is available. This represents the supply. The value is also affected by how much people want it. This represents the demand. Therefore, supply and demand influence the price people pay for goods and services.

For instance, if the supply of a product is high, then the product is not rare. Remember, value is connected to how rare or precious something is. For that reason, the item's price will be low when its supply is high. Likewise, the price of an item increases when it is in short supply, especially if many people want to purchase it.

The more popular or useful an item is, the more people will demand it. Initially, the high demand will result in a short supply of the product. Think about the long lines of hopeful customers that form when a new iPhone or iPad is released. Oftentimes, people go home empty-handed. When that happens, a business eventually increases production to meet the growing demand.

Increased production comes at a cost, though. Companies need to hire more workers and use more materials as they boost their supplies by making more products. To get back some of the money they're spending on additional employee wages and extra materials, businesses often increase the prices of their products.

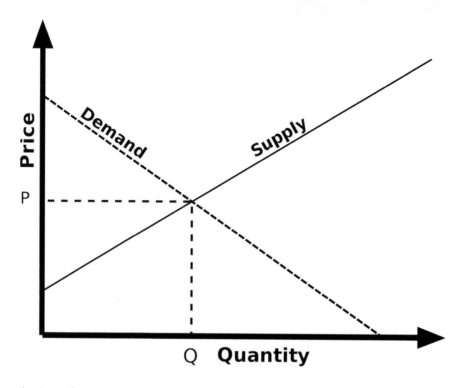

The law of supply and demand determines how buyers and sellers act and react to each other. In general, the law states that when more people want a product or when less of a product is available, the product's price will rise. The goal is to strike a balance between the two forces.

This helps them make a profit. This is the money earned from the sale of a product beyond what it costs to create and sell that product. As long as production costs go up, prices typically will go up as well.

Depending on how strong the demand for goods and services is, and how much money customers can earn or borrow to pay for their purchases, everything may run smoothly in this way for months or even years. Yet, true to the law of supply and demand, higher prices eventually result in decreased demand for a good or service. This happens because people will be either unable or unwilling to pay the higher price.

In 2007, gas prices started to soar. By July, the average price of gasoline was $4.11 per gallon in the United States. People responded by lowering their demand for gas. Rather than drive their own cars, people took public transportation, walked, or joined a carpool. By October 2007, demand had decreased by 10 percent compared to the previous year. By 2009, when the country was in the midst of a recession, gas prices had dropped dramatically.

As gas prices soared in 2007, people found other means of transportation in order to avoid paying high gas prices. This caused reduced demand for gasoline, which ultimately reduced its price.

Price and Wage Stickiness

When demand for goods and services goes down, the market tries to restore balance by slowing down, or contracting. Prices drop, and items go on sale. Production slows down. However, there are some areas of the economy that resist quick correction. Some costs of doing business remain high even as the rest of the economy contracts. These areas are said to be sticky because during periods of economic contraction, they get stuck at expansion levels.

Wages and income are examples of this stickiness. Workers are hired at salary levels that reflect the current economy. If an expansion is under way, then starting wages will be higher than normal. When a slowdown occurs, businesses might offer lower salaries to new employees. However, wages for those who are already employed do not automatically go down. People keep earning the salary that was agreed upon when they were first hired. Companies are more likely to lay off workers than try to reduce sticky wages.

Another example of economic stickiness concerns so-called menu costs. The best example of this type of stickiness is the price list on restaurant menus. Once prices are set and printed on menus or in brochures, businesses cannot easily change them to reflect an economic contraction. The cost of reprinting materials every time the economy changes would cause more damage to a business than simply leaving prices high.

Sticky wages and prices that cannot drop as fast as the economy contracts can cause problems. They can result in companies either not hiring workers or laying off workers, which can worsen the economic contraction.

Economic Shocks

Sometimes, the economy can be performing well and expanding when suddenly something happens. These sorts of events throw the business cycle off course, pushing a country toward recession. These events are called economic shocks. They include natural disasters, such as hurricanes and earthquakes. They also include international conflicts and the introduction of expensive government programs, as well as many other major events.

When shocks occur, money that normally would build up a nation's economy is instead spent taking care of issues surrounding the event. For example, in 2005, Hurricane Katrina devastated New Orleans and much of the Gulf Coast. It resulted in 1,833 deaths and an estimated $125 billion in damage. The US government aided in the cleanup and recovery using funds that it raised through taxes and donations from average citizens. Disaster and humanitarian relief programs are necessary spending, yet they come at a steep cost. When money is

It was estimated that nearly 80 percent of New Orleans was under floodwaters after Hurricane Katrina.

used for economic shocks, it is not used for something else. It's as if you were saving for an Xbox but then wrecked the bike you ride to and from school, so you spent your money on necessary repairs instead.

Inflation

How can having more money in circulation cause a slowdown in the economy? The law of supply and demand affects cash as much as any other good or service. So,

THE PANIC OF 1857

The first recession felt worldwide was the Panic of 1857. There were several factors that contributed to this recession that lasted until 1859. The Ohio Life Insurance and Trust Company collapsed in August 1857. This company was a financial institution that made risky investments that did not make the profits the company imagined. Then, news came out that Ohio Life Insurance and Trust Company members had stolen much of the money used to make the investments. The company had to close its doors. The closure of this major financial institution frightened other banks. This made average citizens worry about their money, so they started withdrawing it from the stock market and from banks. This only caused more issues both at home and abroad.

The telegraph had been created in 1837. It allowed countries across the world to contact each other with more immediacy. Thanks to the telegraph, news of the initial panic spread rapidly, causing other countries to respond. For instance, Britain withdrew its money from US banks, which only further hurt the economy. The panic's impact quickly spread across Europe, South America, Africa, and Asia.

To make matters worse, the SS *Central America* sank in a hurricane in September 1857. This ship was carrying over $50 million in gold that was supposed to be used to back the US dollar. For every dollar in circulation, there was a specific amount of gold to back it. So, for instance, each dollar would be worth an ounce a gold. Without the extra gold to back the dollar, the value of the bills decreased.

All of these issues affected the public's confidence in banking institutions. The more uncertain people were, the more they pulled their money out of these institutions. The more money they pulled out, the easier it was for banks to fail. Although the US economy began to recover in 1859, it wouldn't fully bounce back until the start of the Civil War in 1861.

Eventually, the gold lost when the SS *Central America* sank in 1857 was recovered.

the more money that is in circulation—meaning spread out among the public—the less valuable each bill and coin becomes because of the high supply. When money becomes less valuable, it takes more of it to buy goods and services. This decrease in the value of money is part of the concept of inflation.

Inflation means that prices rise to make up for the value of money going down. For instance, an item may originally be worth one dollar. However, the dollar bill has dropped in value and is now only worth fifty cents. Therefore, it takes two dollar bills to buy the item now. Each dollar has lost half of its former purchasing power, as each dollar can only buy half of what it used to. Meanwhile, prices have doubled. This represents a 100 percent inflation rate.

Governments are primarily responsible for bringing about inflation, which makes trouble for their own economies. Just like individual citizens, countries must have cash to pay for the things they need, including roads and bridges, education, research, the military, and programs such as Medicare. Unlike ordinary people, however, the federal government has a great deal of control over its money supply. When a nation runs short on money, the government can simply print and stamp more. The government can inflate, or increase, the money supply to meet its needs. This trick doesn't last long, though, because eventually the law of supply and demand catches up with the government, in the form of inflation. The more money that's printed, the less each bill is worth.

Inflation's Effect

Inflation's effect on a recession has a lot to do with the behavior of consumers in response to rising prices. Some people will slow down their spending pretty quickly because items are too expensive. Others will keep buying products no matter what the cost because there is a large supply of money still available to them.

Eventually, however, inflation causes people to pull back on spending. This happens because their wages can't keep up with rising prices. Less spending creates a contraction in the business cycle. This causes the economy to cool off and slow down.

Predicting and Identifying Recessions

The first step in determining whether or not the economy is in a recession is to listen to what the economic experts have to say. Even if they don't agree on all the details, they are generally in sync when it comes to the big picture.

CHAPTER 3

ORGANIZATIONS AND INDICATORS

In the United States, there are several different federal agencies responsible for monitoring the economy. These organizations also work to balance out the effects of recessions to help the economy expand again rather than fall into a depression.

The Fed

When it comes to national money matters, the Federal Reserve is the recognized authority within the United States. The Federal Reserve, often referred to simply as the Fed, is the country's central bank. The federal government and all other financial institutions in America use the Fed as their bank, just like you use the local branch of your bank.

Opposite: Although the headquarters of the Federal Reserve, shown here, is in Washington, DC, there are also twelve Federal Reserve banks in cities across the country.

The Fed is an independent government agency watched over by the US Congress. It is also run by a board of directors that are appointed by the president of the United States. As part of its job, the board analyzes the economy and makes policy recommendations. As head of the board, the Fed chairperson delivers a report on the state of the economy to Congress twice a year.

The Fed's job is to oversee the country's banking operations and make sure that the economy stays healthy. It does this by trying to ensure that overall demand equals potential supply within the economy. Therefore, it does not so much determine whether a recession has begun as try to keep normal business-cycle contractions as short as possible.

To accomplish this, the Fed uses interest rates. Interest is the extra amount of cash paid as a sort of fee or service charge to the lender when money is borrowed. The interest charged is usually a certain percentage of the total loan amount. For instance, if someone loaned you thirty dollars with a 10 percent interest rate, you would owe them thirty-three dollars when you paid back your loan.

During periods of rising inflation, the Fed can raise interest rates to keep the economy in check. During recessions, the Fed lowers interest rates. Lower rates essentially mean it costs less to borrow money. The hope is that consumers will feel more comfortable taking out loans at low interest rates. The Fed hopes that these people will then use that money to boost the economy in the form of spending.

The Fed makes money from interest on things like US savings bonds. The Federal Reserve also receives money from interest earned on foreign investments and on loans to banks, as well as services provided to other banks. The Fed turns this money over to the United States Department of the Treasury for safekeeping. The US Department of the Treasury is the government agency responsible for developing policies that manage the economy.

Countries around the world have similar federal agencies and organizations that influence their business cycles. The Bank of Canada, the People's Bank of China, and the European Central Bank (representing countries in the financially linked European Union) are all examples of international institutions that have duties and powers like those of the US Federal Reserve.

The National Bureau of Economic Research and Its Committee

The Fed has control over interest rates, and the United States government determines how much of the country's money is printed. Both of these acts affect contractions in the business cycle. However, the task of declaring a recession is typically left to a nonprofit organization called the National Bureau of Economic Research (NBER).

The NBER has built a solid reputation as a knowledgeable, influential force when it comes to shaping American economic policy and programs. In fact, the federal government often looks to the bureau's Business Cycle Dating Committee. This committee keeps track of economic activity such as the peaks and troughs in the business cycle on a monthly basis. The government uses this information to make the official determination as to whether or not a recession has taken place.

While paying close attention to the GDP, the committee also considers income, employment, and industrial production before announcing that the economy is in recession. Using these economic indicators, the committee identifies when the business cycle has peaked and exactly when it has hit a trough. The time between those two high and low points is what the NBER calls a recession.

Types of Economic Indicators

In order to reach conclusions regarding a recession, the NBER looks at sets of information known as economic indicators. They are called indicators because the data and statistics point out the direction of the economy.

You might think that when a slowdown is involved, indicators would also show a decline, but this is not always

Organizations like the National Bureau of Economic Research use a number of economic indicators to determine whether the United States is in a recession.

the case. Economic indicators can be either procyclic or countercyclic. Procyclic indicators move in the same direction as the business cycle. During a recession, these statistics move downward along with the economy. Retail sales are an example of procyclic indicators. If sales figures are up, then the economy is expanding. When they fall, there is an economic contraction.

Countercyclic indicators, on the other hand, move in the opposite direction of the business cycle. This means that they increase or move upward during a slowdown.

QUICK Q&A

Is the business cycle a fairly regular series of economic ups and downs?

The business cycle does show peaks and troughs in the economy, but it is by no means regular or consistent. Recessions can be long or short, as can the time between them.

When the economy is doing well, usually the stock market does well too. Likewise, during an economic recession, the stock market usually suffers. However, there are better indicators of a recession than the performance of the stock market.

Is the stock market an important indicator in determining whether or not the country is in a recession?

Watching the stock market is helpful in that it reflects economic health and consumers' willingness to invest in the economy. However, it is not the most important indicator. A nation's GDP and unemployment rate give a much better overall picture of an economic slowdown.

Even though recessions are normal, are they terrible for the economy?

How negatively a recession affects the economy depends on how long and deep it is. For instance, during the first two decades of the twenty-first century, aside from the Great Recession, recessions in the United States were fairly short and mild. Remember, recessions can be merely the economy balancing itself after extreme growth. They don't always signal a crisis or disaster.

For instance, the number of people who are unemployed will rise as the business cycle contracts.

Economic indicators are also time-sensitive. They are closely connected to the past, present, or future. Lagging indicators show what has already happened in the business cycle. Coincident indicators give a clear picture of current economic activity. However, the most useful information comes from leading indicators. These statistics indicate what is most likely to happen in the near future. By closely following leading indicators, economists and other advisers are better able to recognize a brewing recession. With this information, they can either try to stop a recession or at least reduce the damage that results from a serious business-cycle contraction.

Examples of Economic Indicators

The GDP is perhaps the most reliable leading indicator. It reveals overall buying and selling patterns on a monthly, quarterly, or yearly basis. As a procyclic indicator, the GDP moves in the same direction as the business cycle. Therefore, during an economic contraction, the GDP decreases. However, GDP isn't the only leading indicator. Declining stock prices may also signal an upcoming recession. Similarly, the consumer price index (CPI) is also a leading indicator. It measures the changes in prices of goods and services over time.

As mentioned before, unemployment figures are countercyclic indicators. As the economy dips into a recession, the unemployment rate increases. The unemployment rate is also a lagging indicator. A high unemployment rate reflects entry into a recession but does not predict one.

Best Indicators

Although there are many ways to gauge the economy through this variety of indicators, not all collections of economic indicators are created equal. Several groups publish indicator lists. However, the most trusted source for reliable data in the United States is the Joint Economic Committee (JEC) of the US Congress. The committee is made up of twenty members. These members include ten senators and ten members of the House of Representatives from both major political parties.

The JEC works with the Council of Economic Advisers. This council is made up of a group of economists who give input to the president on economic policy. Together, the council and the JEC analyze indicators each month in the following seven categories:

- total output, income, and spending
- employment, unemployment, and wages
- production and business activity
- prices

- money, credit, and security markets
- federal finance
- international statistics

Another respected collection of economic statistics is the Leading Economic Index (LEI). These statistics are compiled by the Conference Board, a nonprofit business research organization. The LEI measures business-cycle changes in nine countries, including the United States. The index factors in many things, including the average hours worked each week by manufacturing employees and the number of orders they fill. Similarly, the index considers performance of the stock market and how confident consumers are in the health of their national economies. Taken together, the indicators in the LEI reflect all the factors that influence the GDP. If the leading indicators show a decline for three months in a row, chances are good that the economy will enter a recession within the next twelve months.

Personal Knowledge

In addition to these national and international organizations tracking the economy, you can also watch for signs of a slowdown yourself. There are a number of economic indicators that can act as red flags, warning you that a recession is coming or has already arrived. By listening and watching, you'll have a better idea of the economic situation in the world at large and in your own life.

Responsible spending and borrowing practices help individuals stay financially stable in uncertain economic times.

CHAPTER 4

TWENTY-FIRST-CENTURY RECESSIONS

Recessions have been around for as long as there have been money supplies and the exchange of cash for goods and services. For instance, many historians believe that inflation and a resulting recession were contributing factors to the fall of the Roman Empire. Although modern recessions haven't necessarily gone so far as to topple empires, they have seriously harmed nations' fortunes and affected millions of people.

Late Twentieth-Century Recessions

The late 1980s and early 1990s were an active, complex time for the US economy. The country was dealing with a banking crisis. Hundreds of small savings and loan

Opposite: During the Great Recession, unemployment rose to above 10 percent in 2009. It was the highest unemployment rate the United States had seen in decades. Some people responded by attending fairs in hopes of finding new jobs.

banks were failing, or going out of business, because of corruption. This meant that powerful people involved with the banks were engaged in illegal behavior. Many of these banks had also made too many bad loans. The United States was also shaken by Black Monday on October 19, 1987, when the stock market experienced one of the largest single-day drops in history. Black Monday affected stock trading around the world.

Strangely enough, these events rattled the US economy but did not immediately cause a recession. It would not be until almost three years later that the economy officially entered a recession. According to the Business Cycle Dating Committee, the 1990–1991 economic downturn was due to a decrease in manufacturing production and sales.

Dot-Com Bubble

After the 1990–1991 recession, the US economy experienced renewed expansion. It was being driven mainly by what was then a new business sector—internet-based companies. Buying and selling online became very popular. Existing retail businesses found they could increase their sales by using the internet. Hoping to take advantage of this situation and make a lot of money, businesspeople created hundreds of companies that specialized exclusively in online sales and computer technology. These were known as dot-coms because the new companies often had ".com" at the end of their names, which is internet shorthand for "commerce."

Many investors bought stock in these new ventures. They believed that dot-coms would make large profits. This would cause their stock value to increase as well. Heavy investing created what is known as a stock bubble. Bubbles happen when the price of stock in a certain business sector rises rapidly. Sometimes this rapid growth happens regardless of the company's actual worth or the value of its products. The increased demand for the stock inflates the value of it and the perceived value and health of the company.

In their rush to make money, the owners of many dot-coms hadn't created very good business plans. Even worse, some had not even created any actual products to sell. They were simply selling the promise of a product that would eventually be offered and sold. Many of these companies built on flimsy foundations soon folded. Some companies with strong foundations, however, found that there wasn't enough demand for all the products sold online. The supply of dot-coms far exceeded demand for their services, so company values declined.

By 2001, the technology stock bubble had burst. Stock prices fell, spending decreased, and many more internet companies went out of business. The result was a stock

When the dot-com bubble burst, investors lost millions of dollars.

market drop, a decline in the GDP, and an increase in the unemployment rate as thousands of dot-com workers lost their jobs. This series of events triggered the first twenty-first-century recession.

The recession was further affected by the shock of the September 11 terrorist attacks on New York City and Washington, DC, in 2001. Even after all this turmoil, the slowdown was relatively mild. According to the NBER, it lasted only eight months.

Housing and Credit Issues

Following that first recession, many Americans took advantage of low interest rates. These interest rates had been lowered by the Fed to kick-start the economy after the 2001 recession. When interest rates are low, people are more willing to take out loans. Usually, people are especially encouraged to take out mortgages. These are loans from the bank for houses. As the Fed lowered its interest rates, banks also lowered their mortgage interest rates and lending requirements. They even made subprime mortgages available to people who were credit risks.

Subprime mortgages are given to borrowers that do not have good credit ratings. Each borrower, whether it's an individual or an organization, has a credit rating.

The hundreds of thousands of foreclosures on houses affected real people, who were being forced out of their houses.

This number estimates the borrower's ability to honor financial commitments. The rating is based on the borrower's financial history. For instance, a person's credit score will reflect that individual's history of paying bills on time and in full. If someone has bad credit, it means that person perhaps failed to pay a number of bills on time or never paid them at all.

Offering subprime mortgages to people with bad credit is very risky for the lender or bank. In fact, these types of mortgages are so risky that historically they were generally avoided. Usually, when they were given, they came at a high interest rate for the borrower, to help offset the bank's risk. They were also carefully insured in case the borrower could not pay back the loan. This meant that the lender would be covered by another company so that it wouldn't lose its money if the borrower could not pay. In the 2000s, however, subprime mortgages increased dramatically.

It became so easy to buy real estate that many people took advantage of the easy money banks were offering. These individuals even put up their homes as collateral to borrow even more money from the bank to buy luxury items like boats, expensive cars, and second homes. Collateral is valuable property that a borrower agrees to give to a lender if payments are not made on a loan.

As people purchased more houses, increasing demand, the value of houses went up. As the values went up, so did real estate prices. Unfortunately, people's incomes didn't rise at the same rate. Soon, houses cost more than the average consumer could afford. By 2007, home sales dropped and borrowers defaulted on loans, meaning they failed to pay them back on time or at all.

Complicating matters was the fact that groups of risky subprime mortgages were offered as special investment opportunities known as securities. Basically, outside investors gave banks the funds to cover these shaky loans, expecting in return to share the money from interest when the loans were repaid. When subprime borrowers defaulted, the investors lost money along with the banks. This caused a shake-up in stock markets worldwide, since international banks and investors had purchased these securities. Even those investors who had stayed away from the securities became nervous. They were afraid their stocks and other investments would fail just like the subprime securities had. As a result, they made fewer new investments. They weren't even investing in relatively safe and healthy companies and projects.

Several indicators seemed to suggest that the economy was in a recession after these housing and credit difficulties. Stock market trading and the GDP dropped. Jobs were cut in the real estate, construction, and finance sectors. As a result, unemployment rose. Additionally, consumer confidence was very low. This leading indicator gauges how people feel about the economy and the security of their income. It is based on a survey of five thousand households. Low consumer confidence predicts a reduction in consumer spending. During this time, a majority of the Americans surveyed believed that they were in the middle of a recession. For that reason, they were no longer spending their money.

Finally, in December 2007, consumers' suspicions were confirmed. The United States entered a recessionary period. It would come to be known as the Great Recession, and it would have a worldwide effect.

The Great Recession

The Great Recession, according to the NBER, lasted from December 2007 until June 2009. The period caused widespread damage. For instance, in 2009, 140 US banks failed. These banks failed because of borrowers' inabilities to repay loans. Because of these bank failures, many people could not find institutions to loan them money for houses or businesses. As a result, people could not afford to buy homes. This meant further drops in employment opportunities for construction workers and in the financial sector.

"We've rented out the kitchen for extra money to pay the mortgage. Want to eat out?"

This cartoon captures how desperate people were just to keep their homes during the Great Recession.

In general, unemployment rates rose. At the beginning of the recession, in February 2008, the unemployment rate was 4.8 percent. By October 2009, unemployment had risen to 10.2 percent. This was the country's highest unemployment rate since April 1983. Additionally, with so many people losing their jobs and businesses not hiring, people who had purchased houses found it

TWENTY-FIRST CENTURY GLOBAL RECESSION

Countries around the world felt the effects of the Great Recession, which started in the United States. This happened because international economies are closely linked through global trade in the twenty-first century. When the US economy suffered, other international economies took a hit. Especially hard hit were economies in Japan and European countries like Greece, Iceland, Latvia, Portugal, and Spain. These countries suffered because of their close economic ties with the United States.

The global financial crisis came at a particularly difficult time for Greece. The country had been underestimating its deficits for several years before the crisis. Deficits happen when a country's government spends more money than it takes in through taxes and other income. To make up the difference, the country borrows money, perhaps from banks or foreign governments. In order to keep the country running in the early part of the century, Greece's government borrowed lots of money. When global markets began to collapse in 2008, Greece struggled to pay back its loans. Its financial struggles continued for at least a decade.

difficult to pay back their loans. In 2008 alone, nearly one million people lost their homes.

In response, the government poured around $4 trillion into the financial sector to boost the economy. Similarly, it reduced interest rates to near zero. Although all of these measures helped pull the country out of the recession, it would still take both the US economy and economies around the world affected by the US financial collapse years to recover.

PREPARATION AND RECOVERY

Predicting a recession is tricky business. As part of the normal business cycle, recessions occur in the United States, on average, every five to ten years. The NBER states that in recent years, economic slowdowns have been cropping up less frequently than in decades past. According to the International Monetary Fund, global recessions occur about every eight to ten years. Beyond these facts, however, no one can be certain when the business cycle will contract. Similarly, it is hard to predict how severe a given contraction may be. There are ways, however, to prepare.

How to Prepare: Fiscal Policy

Governments can introduce measures aimed at minimizing the effects of a recession before it starts. These measures

Opposite: Regardless of whether the economy is expanding or contracting, consumers should be mindful of overspending.

usually take the form of policies that affect the country from year to year. Economic policy is an attempt by a nation's government or central bank to influence the movements of the business cycle.

There are two categories of policy that directly affect the economy: fiscal policy and monetary policy. Fiscal policy is the responsibility of lawmakers and other government officials. In the United States, this includes the president and Congress. With fiscal policy, the government adds money to the economy in order to increase the demand for goods and services. The thinking is that people will spend more when there is more money available to them. This spending stimulates the economy.

Reducing taxes and increasing government spending are the two main fiscal policies used to insert money into the economy. The government receives taxpayer dollars through yearly income tax filings and sales tax on purchases. The lowering of taxes leaves more money in taxpayers' pockets. Tax rebates, in which the government sends checks to taxpayers as a way to get them to spend more, may also occur during a recession. This tactic was used in both 2001 and 2008.

Government spending also stimulates the economy. This spending can take the form of direct spending on goods and services or through projects such as road and bridge construction. Government spending jump-starts

Federally funded projects, such as the building of roads or schools, help lower unemployment rates and fix the economy during recessions.

production in various business sectors, creating more jobs and greater demand for goods and services. Money makes its way back into the economy through increased GDP and personal income.

How to Prepare: Monetary Policy

Monetary policy is the responsibility of a country's central bank. In the United States, that's the Federal Reserve. The goal of monetary policy is to stabilize employment levels and prices. The Fed does this by influencing the availability of money and the affordability of borrowing and credit. To accomplish this, more money needs to be injected into the economy.

The Fed has three major tools that help set monetary policy in motion. Open market operations involve the

A FEW MORE FACTS

War can be good for the economy.

Throughout history, wars have been known to stimulate the economy. In fact, many historians believe that military spending during World War II helped the United States rebound from the Great Depression. Feeding, clothing, and otherwise taking care of the troops pumps money into a nation's GDP. Manufacturing weapons creates jobs in the industrial and defense sectors.

The production of supplies for World War II put Americans to work and helped lift the economy out of the Great Depression.

Over time, however, conflicts can be a drain on the economy. The money spent on defense gets moved away from other areas of the economy and business sectors. Sometimes, governments even have to borrow money from other countries in order to be able to pay their war expenses. This can increase national debt.

Government subsidies help failing business sectors.

When a company is not able to make a profit, it is very discouraging for that business's owner and its employees. When whole groups of companies in a particular business sector don't turn a profit, it is bad news for the entire economy. When this happens, the government turns to a form of spending known as subsidies.

A subsidy is a government payment meant to encourage economic activity in a business or business sector that provides a necessary or unique product. When lack of profit threatens such an industry (like agriculture, steel, or automobile manufacturing), the government supports, or subsidizes, it with cash. This helps lower production costs and keeps the various companies within the industry in business.

buying and selling of government securities such as bonds and treasury bills. Citizens buy these bonds and bills with the government's promise that, after holding on to them for a certain period of time, they will be worth more than the original price paid. It's like buying stock, only you're investing in the government instead of an individual company. Because they are backed by the US government, bonds and treasury bills are considered safer investments than the stock market.

The money that the government raises by selling securities can be spent on all kinds of programs that would otherwise have to be funded by the raising of taxes. During a recession, the government may buy back the securities it has sold. The money the government pays goes directly to the person who bought the securities. Most people will invest at least some of the money they earn from the sale of their securities back into the government. They may also use some of the money to buy things, which pumps much-needed money back into the economy.

Another monetary policy tool is a reduced interest rate on loans from the Fed to other banks. Lower interest rates generally encourage borrowing.

The Fed incorporates its third monetary policy tool by adding to or reducing reserves. Reserves represent the money banks set aside from deposits as a security measure. This is a way to make sure banks have enough money on hand to cover depositor activity. For instance, the reserve covers the withdrawals individuals might make from their account at an ATM.

Banks in the United States, including the Fed, are required to keep a percentage of their total deposits in reserve. Money above and beyond the reserve requirement is available for lending, which stimulates the economy. To make sure this happens, the Fed may reduce the reserve rate requirement. So, if a bank has deposits equaling $1 million and the reserve rate is 20 percent, the reserve of cash that would have to be on hand would be $200,000. At a lower reserve rate of 10 percent, only $100,000 has to be held in reserve. The extra $100,000 deposited in the bank is now freed up for lending and the eventual spending or investing that will strengthen an economy.

Price Caps

Good economic policy can help shorten a recession and ease the problems associated with a slowdown. Bad economic policy, on the other hand, can actually bring on a recession. One example of the latter type of policy involves price controls.

Price controls are a legal limit on how high prices in a certain business sector can rise. The limit is also called a cap. Governments have used price controls frequently in the past to fight inflation. At first glance, it would seem that any policy aimed at keeping prices affordable would be a good thing. However, while price controls may help in the short term, they can disrupt the business cycle.

The reason has to do with the effect that fixing prices at a set amount has on production. Placing a cap on the price of a good or service keeps the cost low for consumers, which increases demand. As a result, businesses need more workers and materials to keep up with the increased demand. However, when price controls are in place, companies are not able to set higher prices that let them make a profit after increased expenses. Without that profit, they can't afford new employees or other higher production costs associated with increased production. For these reasons, the supply of the original price-controlled item decreases, even though demand from the public is still high. This negatively affects the natural flow of supply and demand.

Individual Financial Health

We've seen how governments handle a recession through economic policy. Now let's take a look at some personal policy measures you can take that will help you cope with an economic slowdown. While there's no way to become absolutely recession-proof, there are commonsense steps that you can take to protect your wealth and purchasing power.

Key factors to surviving recessions are responsible spending habits and savings. Responsible spending habits mean making sure that you're spending wisely on any goods and services like clothing or movie theater tickets. This responsible spending will leave you with more money in savings. The more money you have in savings, the easier it will be to ride the highs and lows of the economic cycle.

Working Together

A country's financial health is dependent on both its citizens and its government officials. Citizens need to pay close attention to the law of supply and demand in their own lives. They can try their best to live within their means. They can also encourage their government and elected officials to do the same. Both governments and ordinary citizens can best fight a recession by remaining calm, careful, and reasonable in their actions and reactions.

GLOSSARY

business cycle The natural way the economy works, through a pattern of ups (expansions) and downs (contractions).

central bank A country's primary money authority.

countercyclic An economic indicator that moves in the opposite direction of the business cycle.

depression A prolonged period of very low economic activity; a severe recession.

economic indicators Data and statistics that provide information about the health of the economy and the business cycle.

economic shocks Unpredictable or unplanned events that affect the economy, like natural disasters or international conflicts.

exports Goods and services a country sells to other nations.

globalization The connections between businesses and marketplaces around the world.

gross domestic product (GDP) The total value of all goods and services produced in the country in a given period of time, such as a month, a quarter (three months), or a year.

gross national product (GNP) The total value of all goods and services produced by a country, both domestically and abroad, during a given period.

imports Goods and services that a country buys from other nations.

inflation A rise in the price level of goods and services.

interest The extra amount paid as a fee or service charge to the lender when money is borrowed, usually a certain percentage of the total loan amount.

peak The high point of the business cycle.

procyclic An economic indicator that moves in the same direction as the business cycle.

recession When the economy experiences a slowdown, or contraction.

stickiness The condition when prices or wages can't change as quickly as the business cycle.

subprime loan An amount lent to a borrower with a weak credit history.

supply and demand A natural law that maps out how buyers and sellers act on their own and react to each other. In general, the law states that when more people want a product, or when less of a product is available, the product's price will rise.

trough The low point in the business cycle.

FURTHER INFORMATION

Books

Kallen, Stuart A. *The Great Recession*. Understanding World History. San Diego: ReferencePoint Press, 2014.

Loria, Laura. *Inflation, Deflation, and Unemployment*. Understanding Economics. New York: Rosen Publishing, 2019.

O'Hara, Scarlett, and Margaret Parrish, eds. *Heads Up Money*. New York: DK Publishing, 2016.

Owoeye, Erica. *Understanding Supply and Demand*. 21st-Century Economics. New York: Cavendish Square, 2019.

Websites

The Library of Economics and Liberty: High School Economic Topics

http://www.econlib.org/library/Topics/HighSchool/HighSchoolTopics.html

This website provides an extensive glossary containing economics terms and definitions.

National Employment Monthly Update

http://www.ncsl.org/research/labor-and-employment/national-employment-monthly-update.aspx

This website provides month-by-month information about the employment rate for the past ten years.

Videos

Here's What Caused the Great Recession

https://www.youtube.com/watch?v=yM0uonkloXY

This video explains the subprime mortgage crisis, the burst of the housing bubble, and the impact of these events.

Nominal vs. Real GDP

https://www.youtube.com/watch?v=rGqhTQyY6g4

This video explains the differences between nominal and real GDP using examples.

Organizations

Bank of Canada
234 Wellington Street
Ottawa, ON K1A 0G9
Canada
(800) 303-1282
Website: http://www.bank-banque-canada.ca

Created in 1934, the Bank of Canada is the country's central bank. Like the Federal Reserve in the United States, the Bank of Canada is responsible for the management of Canada's money and monetary policies.

Board of Governors of the Federal Reserve System
20th Street and Constitution Avenue NW
Washington, DC 20551
(202) 452-3000
Website: http://www.federalreserve.gov

The Federal Reserve System serves as the United States' central bank. Its headquarters are in Washington, DC, and there are twelve reserve banks located in major US cities.

Bureau of Economic Analysis
4600 Silver Hill Road
Suitland, MD 20746
(301) 278-9004
Website: https://www.bea.gov

This federal agency provides up-to-date, accurate, and nonbiased economic statistics and data.

National Bureau of Economic Research
1050 Massachusetts Avenue
Cambridge, MA 02138
(617) 868-3900
Website: http://www.nber.org

The NBER is a nonprofit research organization dedicated to promoting a greater understanding of how the US economy works.

Treasury Board of Canada Secretariat
90 Elgin Street, 8th Floor
Ottawa, ON K1A 0R5
Canada
(877) 636-0656
Website: http://www.tbs-sct.gc.ca

This government body provides oversight of financial management functions in other departments and agencies.

SELECTED BIBLIOGRAPHY

Christie, Les. "Foreclosures Up a Record of 81% in 2008." CNNMoney.com, January 15, 2009. https://money.cnn.com/2009/01/15/real_estate/millions_in_foreclosure.

Clayton, Gary E. *Economics: Principles and Practices.* Westerville, OH: Glencoe/McGraw-Hill, 2004.

"Explaining Greece's Debt Crisis." *New York Times,* June 17, 2016. https://www.nytimes.com/interactive/2016/business/international/greece-debt-crisis-euro.html.

Gandel, Stephen. "Survival Strategies: Recession-Proof Your Life." CNNMoney.com, February 27, 2008. http://money.cnn.com/2008/02/08/pf/recession_proof.moneymag.

Gereffi, Gary. "The Global Economy: Organization, Governance, and Development." In *Handbook of Economic Sociology*, edited by Neil J. Smelser and Richard Swedberg. Princeton, NJ: Princeton University Press, 2004.

Gross, Daniel. "Why It's Worse Than You Think." *Newsweek,* June 7, 2008. https://www.newsweek.com/economy-why-its-worse-you-think-90989.

Hennerich, Heather. "What Does the Fed Look At to Predict Recessions?" Federal Reserve Bank of St. Louis, February 14, 2018. https://www.stlouisfed.org/open-vault/2018/february/fed-predict-recessions.

Maybury, Richard J. *Whatever Happened to Penny Candy?* Placerville, CA: Bluestocking Press, 2004.

"The Recession and Recovery in Perspective." Federal Reserve Bank of Minneapolis, October 20, 2018. https://www.minneapolisfed.org/publications/special-studies/recession-in-perspective?sc_device=Default.

Reynolds, Alan. "Economic Hysteria." *New York Post*, April 11, 2008. http://www.nypost.com/seven/04112008/postopinion/opedcolumnists/economic_hysteria_106074.htm.

Schiffman, Betsy. "'Pervasive' Recession Won't Repeat Dot-Com Bust, Experts Say." *Wired*, March 2008. http://www.wired.com/techbiz/startups/news/2008/03/dotcom_repeat.

"Sunken Treasure from Gold Rush–Era Shipwreck to Go on Display." CBS News, February 20, 2018. https://www.cbsnews.com/news/sunken-treasure-ship-of-gold-ss-central-america.

"Today in History – August 24." Library of Congress, October 15, 2018. https://www.loc.gov/item/today-in-history/august-24.

Wearden, Graeme. "Greece Debt Crisis: Timeline." *Guardian*, May 5, 2010. https://www.theguardian.com/business/2010/may/05/greece-debt-crisis-timeline.

INDEX

Page numbers in **boldface** refer to images.

ABOUT THE AUTHOR

Chet'la Sebree is a writer, editor, and researcher. She has written and edited several books for Cavendish Square Publishing, including one on the Great Depression. She has degrees in English and creative writing from the University of Richmond and American University, respectively. She is from the Mid-Atlantic region.